Unlikely Vessels

Pamela Leach

Unlikely Vessels

Acknowledgements

I am most grateful to all who have mentored, supported and encouraged me in my poetry. These include Helen Swain, Robyn Mathison, Liz Winfield, Mark Macleod, Alison McConnell, Betty McKenzie-Tubb, Jan Colville, Pat Firkin, Tony Brennan, Laura Murray and my friends at Hobart Women's Poetry Oasis, The Domain Writers, Grove Poets, the Fellowship of Australian Writers (Tasmania) and Varuna, the National Writer's House.

Dedication

This volume is for refugees who have come Australia by boat and not received their entitlement to warm welcome, human rights and dignity, and for those who have extended hands of friendship.
It carries my sorrow, solidarity and gratitude to First Peoples who have been displaced and dishonoured by seafarers, yet remain gracious, generous and hopeful.
These poems come with love to Katherine who opens my eyes and heart to write, a constant and devoted partner through every weather.

Unlikely Vessels
ISBN 978 1 76109 567 2
Copyright © text Pamela Leach 2023
Cover photo by Pamela Leach – Lettes Bay

First published 2023 by
GINNINDERRA PRESS
PO Box 3461 Port Adelaide 5015
www.ginninderrapress.com.au

Contents

I Casting Off
- Departure — 11
- Blood vessel — 12
- Island — 13
- Pilgrimage — 14
- The cradle she rocks — 15
- Dream on — 16
- Nesting at sea — 17
- Oasis — 18
- Yarning with Walt — 19

II Adrift
- Ferry commons — 27
- Incantation — 28
- New order — 29
- Passage — 30
- Selfie — 31
- Sailing trapeze — 32
- Unborn or dead — 33
- Lunar — 34
- The octopus's mending — 35
- Reunion — 36
- Piñada — 37
- Double-ender — 38

III Into Port
- The shallows — 41
- On the verge — 42
- Ordinary miracles — 43
- First — 44
- No return — 45
- The end of the road — 46
- One stroke — 47

Never mind I'm fourteen	48
Finian's call	49
On the charts	50
Anybody's god	51

IV Excursion

Centrifugal	55
A thousand miles from care	56
Brimming vessels	57
Sydney experiments	58
Manly Ferry, 1939	59
Isle of Man Caravan Club	60
Lessons from the Bellevue	61
Barging in	62
Recall	64
Begging buckets	65

V Rough Passage

Laws of the sea	69
Corked	70
Terminus	71
Sorry to have missed you	72
Flags of convenience	73
Reading room exclusive	74
People of the ferry	75
Submariner	78
The lure	80

VI Foundering

Blowhole	83
Secret	84
The ship-breaker	85
Hey poem!	87
Knots for beginners	88
'I'll see you then'	90

VII Pilot Station
　Subject to change　　　　　　　　　　　　　97
　Late running lights　　　　　　　　　　　　99
　A marked man　　　　　　　　　　　　　100
　On Hebe Reef　　　　　　　　　　　　　101
　Pendant buoy 1830–1960　　　　　　　　103
　Beach bone　　　　　　　　　　　　　　104
　Schoolhouse　　　　　　　　　　　　　 105
　Night sailing　　　　　　　　　　　　　 107
　Brush　　　　　　　　　　　　　　　　108
　Ship in a bottle　　　　　　　　　　　　 109

VIII Bruny Island Ferry
　Mirage　　　　　　　　　　　　　　　　113
　Nautical draughts　　　　　　　　　　　 114
　Hydraulic force　　　　　　　　　　　　115
　Deckhands　　　　　　　　　　　　　　116
　Picture postcard　　　　　　　　　　　　117
　Our Kettering　　　　　　　　　　　　　118
　Sunday at the Beeswing　　　　　　　　　119
　Missing out　　　　　　　　　　　　　　120
　Albatross　　　　　　　　　　　　　　　121
　The limits　　　　　　　　　　　　　　 122
　Bruny Island　　　　　　　　　　　　　 123
　Bucket list　　　　　　　　　　　　　　 124
　White lies　　　　　　　　　　　　　　 125
　Long weekend　　　　　　　　　　　　 126

About the poet　　　　　　　　　　　　　　127

I

Casting Off

Departure

In the dawn belly of our whale, we are founding a city,
    animals, campervans, big people, little people,
lost people. A car alarm wails, sparks cacophony.
    The air's lubed with diesel fumes, bulkheads throb,
the wheeled are unashamed nose-to-tail strays.
    Above the dim hold, light glares.

White sea, sky, smoke soften bushfires' scorch. Stragglers
    hunch at the rail. Tasmania, our home movie, fades.
This ship is packed with islanders bracing for a mainland
    Christmas, car boots jammed with parcels and
puddings. Slabs of warm Cascade beer thrum on electric tools.
    Lounge uncertainty's masked with newsy papers,

'Ex-brothel Raid After Carjacking', 'How Triplets Healed
    My Broken Heart'. Sunrise blusters at itself between
facing widescreens. Bush smoke reminds the hosts of how
    to glaze a ham with Coke if you've seventy dollars
for a ham, none over for brown sugar, Keen's mustard
    and a pinch of cloves. Pretzelled into lounge chairs,

we sleep off late-night packing. Truckers sprawl wide-kneed,
    numbing the hours away from their security-cabs.
They're not sure Christmas with the kids and missus will
    be sweeter than open country and roadhouse tucker,
where no one blinks if you order double chips, jacket potatoes,
    and a boat of gravy to drown your heart.

Blood vessel

Show me a ship, I'll show you a culture
says the seer, archaeologist, bald monk in her saffron.
A ferry's a ship, polaroid trip, feature film feast
for people-watchers, scholars of human conditions.
A ferry's a ouija board babbling as sea levels rise.

Show me a ferry, I'll show you culture, blind spots
and smears, open decks, whiffs of urine and usury.
Show me a ferry, I'll show you lonely, averted eyes
staring at translucent toe scuffs, bags of claptrap,
seeking fresh sight into all they are, are not.

A ferry's a time capsule, like we made with Mum's
coffee canister at the dawn of instant. A safety pin,
dead light globe, new penny, a grudging iced vovo,
hardly licked, cylindrical buried SOS, fragments
from a childhood none of us would survive intact.

A ferry's a ship of hours, CCTV, taste, smellivision,
more real than Netflix. We dive into wounds,
ours and theirs, telltale as crumbs caught in a fridge
seal. As a rock lobster twiddles pincers, I pen
seagoing poetry lazing in a gently warming pot.

Island

It's all about getting from this little island
I call home to that bigger island where they say
it all happens. This ten-storey ferry, high-rise tall ship
sets sail – well, engines – to that mysterious shore.
It's a deed more confronting than being an I-land,
just a rough line of coast turning to glimpse itself
with surprise, as a dog gleefully meets her own tail,
barking 'What, WHAT, are you doing, behind
and before me?' She sets to chasing it, we all do.
The big north island meets the boomer tail
of its own shore in a bay I'll never see. Australia gazes
on that thundering white beach, shouting 'Fa-a-ah-ck,
after all this time, here I am.' But is it more for an island
than for me? Under the skylight's glare, I face
my rumpled face, snarling bedhead, and chuckle,
'Jiminy, after all this time, here I am.'

Pilgrimage

If you board the ferry
resistant,   many do,
but get carried along
all are,   let yourself go
to the edge, open rail and be
sleek   on the surface,
tossed in impossible's agony,
almost walking   brave on water.
You may find *ruach*,
spirit-wind   stings your cheek.

In the tepid air of the lounge,
great leveller   of contempt,
communion may waft among
pie eaters,   passengers
with nothing and everything
in their eyes,   in their minds.
You may find yourself by chance,
sheer accident   on a course
unexpected, a wonder-journey.

The cradle she rocks

On the *Spirit of Tasmania II*

This *Spirit*'s intense, got her sleeves
        rolled up, crossing's a routine smoko.
She's a working gal, wears greasy overalls
        if she wears anything at all.
Her tats offer sobering life advice: 'Caution,
        Wet Surfaces', 'Remember your Deck'
'Take Meds with You', and 'Mind your Head'.
        This girl's resonant, hums her tune
over clank and slam. Across her skin, steely lugs
        are beauty spots, piercings
for tethers to hold this vast wheelie-cargo
        in place if mutiny tries
to seduce the night. Down here, it's ghostly,
        bracketting oily hours of loading, unloading
wily vehicles, menageries, their people. Few mull over
        The *Spirit*'s higher power, upward heave,
not of decks, ramps, hydraulics, but her curvy buoyancy
        against gravity's cheeky force.
She keeps the upper hand so we might suspend fear,
        glide easy in this cradle she rocks.

Dream on

A ten-hour ferry ride's
    a cheap cruise if you look at it
        that way. Don't miss anything.
Queue for the cinema,
    no more gala than a home DVD.

Queue twice to dine,
    don't miss steamed bain-marie meals
        – not included –
and the mystery-meat carvery
    where you'll carry your own tray.

Queue too at the bar
    – no table service –
        but the stools are black vinyl
cones, ready for double scoops of bum,
    fitting for bespoke plastic holidays.

Ferry passengers don't cruise,
    we don't miss fine china,
        the clink of crystal, rustling starch,
spit and polish of stewards.
    Melamine too has its retro cachet.

Just when we're glutted with pretence,
    the ship's shop, a tomato sauce desert,
        sells out of meat pies,
and passengers scrape the last gossipy barnacle
    from their dented hulls.

There's a blessed bump at the north end
    of endless Port Phillip Bay where
        the concrete mouth of the Yarra pouts.
Sweet release drains us slowly
    into beachfront gridlock.

Nesting at sea

Something about the rolling hum of a ferry
sailing Bass Strait, any great body, slips passengers

into horizontal gear, animal need. Seasoned travellers
with money take cabins, micro-views to steady stomachs.

They shroud their bodies in starched sheets, are gone
a full hour before we pull out of Devonport.

Ferry-virgins do not pack scroggin or glacé ginger
all the way from Buderim. They'll learn at sea why

emergency rations are a must, how the jaw wants placating.
We penny-pinchers board early, bag liminal corners

hoping to stretch out under radar's rules. Heads burrow
beneath coats, a flutter that faceless, we broach no discussion.

The habit of nesting at sea is crude but certain
among strangers pressed together, defences lowered.

Curiosity's dulled by thrum and roll. Heads drop
into chins, loll back, snores crackle. The restive few

face slack, wobbling wattles fit for turkeys
and well-hung uvulas, too-pink fleshy intimacies.

Oasis

There are shadows resistant to the prying public,
flitting from car to seclusion, to cabins whose
glass eye inverts truth, alleges a moving world,

steady oval frame. In this pigeonhole, suspended
between agendas, I may become most myself.
I'd choose marooning here over the pack-hold

of most family reunions. I'm provisioned,
thick novel to navigate, date bars for hard tack.
My laptop's perched, powered up to receive verse.

Even the Little Prince found it hard to get lost
on a micro-planet but my feral mind's a tearaway,
pumped for wild on this incy-wincy footprint.

If premium bulkheads stifle, spray-slick decks
are vacant now, froth below in foment, glimpses
of kangaroo, angel phlegm, smiling moon.

Station Pier finally rescues us into ferry flotsam
and fairy floss, as it has other desperadoes,
migrants from oceans of plight, flight and fancy.

To ride the ferry is to wade into the mix.
Who needs holidays on pounding shelly shores
where vacating poets risk only rust?

Yarning with Walt

A chat with poet Walt Whitman, borrowing phrases from his 'Crossing Brooklyn Ferry'. Whitman was moved by Quaker (Friends') witness of god-in-everyone, ministries of all, thriving together in this earthly home toward an emancipated future.

i. A cloud of witnesses

Not in swaying leaves of grass we meet, but on this ferry
    I am with you. Just as you stand and lean on the rail,
Walt, I am still, yet hurried into slicing slap and gurgle,
    refreshed by the river's gladness, by our ferry commons.
A cloud of witnesses we poets are, dumb, beautiful ministers
    to each other on shore, at sea. Gulls too preach truths
to us as they cavort, glistening yellow lighting up parts
    of their bodies, leaving the rest in shadow.

My river's confettied with blossoms, white wake
    left by the passage of this red-ripe ferry. We're both
bound for apple isles, mine Tasmania, yours Manhattan.
    Lyrics intimate, pedantic, ripple and run as one.
Yet ferrying is neither sport nor prayer at core, but trade.
    In this floating market I find you, Walt,
marooned to face your own spectres – wolf, snake, hog –
    while feeding workaday and free-spirited passengers,
adding a warp of value to each cardboard ticket.

The scallop-edged waves in the twilight, the ladled cups,
    vapour as it flies in fleeces tinged with violet,
your watercolour poems are fluid animation. I see, reflected
    below, centrifugal spokes of light haloing your head.
My words eddy down from this spray-veiled deck
    to the same mirror, splicing this crossing into verse.
To these crowds, their patter, just as to water's libretto,
    you and I query, 'What is it then between us?'

ii. Your gaze

Friend Walt, we all seek to borrow your gaze. I plunge in,
    slither between molecules, questing for it.
Once I found the Mississippi birthing up north, drawling
    country tunes while mosquitos licked their chops
at the feast of me. That rivulet knew nothing yet
    of St Louis' Blues, New Orleans' creole pepper,
the must-dance of Zydeco. Rivers grow old round the mouth,
    where floating's a sweeping passion. In words I drift
to find my bearings. On some cusp, I hunger for instants,
    my Dacron luffing against your drum-tight canvas.

iii. The old knot

You Friend are more curious to me than you suppose.
    I approach you from public housing towers' sour halls,
through camera-eyes of gated estates. Riding waves
    shoulder-to-shoulder, breaking bread together,
more richly serves this human tack than drowning
    each in private freedom's welter.

Walt, it is not upon you alone the dark patches fall.
    I too knit the old knot of contrariety till I'm snagged.
As you fray, so I corrode, chips of me join ice floes,
    clinking in breakneck current, thirst chasing salty sea.
In time we all melt. No ship worth its name stays dry.

iv. Glassy sea

I have my own pitch nights, graveyard watches.
    At fourteen, you were a weekday printer's devil,
I a petty officer on weekends, school holidays.
    Playing grown-up at the helm I nearly wrecked
our brigantine, its child-crew of twenty-seven.
    Red-twin stars, some newfangled Mars, followed
this tall ship, near becalmed. Until in my soft head – aha,
    that hum is a freighter looming, collision pending.

Still now I cringe, the almost-crush, fissures crying
    into holds where anchor chains coil oily. Breathless
summer night, the freighter's crew sleeps, it ploughs ahead
    on autopilot. I belt out commands. Yardarms creak,
sails waft and follow, we veer into wake's wobble, clanking,
    near swamped by the beast. Below, sleepers tossed
in bunks cry out. This cruising out of time, stubborn
    post-digital navigation by sextant blends charm
with primal risk, exposing more than pastel curl of blue
    and yellow charts, a solo pencil plotting our course.

v. On the dawn pier

Most days we poets hunch over debris, pan and sieve
    until we spy some flash within. Dark patches fall
the better to feel the stars, aurora's maypole ribbons,
    know songs of ourselves lapping supple on skin.
It should be easy to keep faith with this universe.
    Like us the sun commutes, finds east, waits smartly
on the dawn pier, collar up, for the first boat.
    Or is it tide's moon-pull that makes me porous
to your glories strung like beads?

vi. Winged things

Once our hope to float was madness. When that Brooklyn
    Bridge you dreaded hung, Walt, fevered men
and women left salted sea for suspension then open air –
    to coast and claw and kill. Louder than a cicada eisteddfod,
vessels fly now, roaring raucous, offending nature in flight.
    Crowds ride aloft, eleven abreast. Cocooned in blankets,
newspapers, drink, they jostle as in any ferry, same old
    laughing, gnawing, sleeping, seeking ease of home
aboard. You didn't predict us pressing every limit, not settling
    for basic bounty, not leaving as much, as good for others.
And horrors, Friend – I'm among the frequent flyers.

Our aerial fears are simple, not crash or fire but virus,
    lateness, lost luggage. Sky-ships don't tack or flap
but wheel in circles, fleet above clouds, spinning
    perverse beauty. Each seat's a pod, human chrysalis
awaiting not just transport but transmutation. A century on,
    curious questionings still stir as we fly. Winged things
incubate hope, blow bubbles into workers' weary heads.

In America some fly to buy bread, milk, diesel-rich coffee,
    commuting to work, to hunt, to war. This may shock you –
some fly for fear of strolling streets in your guns-for-hire land.
    Toddlers shoot their mums bang-dead, cruel wide-eyed
crimes. We know the power of specks – dandelion seeds waft
    to Philly on a hundred tufty filaments. Pushing limits
like you, like Mohammed too I plea, beg to see Gabriel's power.
    I also faint at a glimpse of one soaring, endless feather.

vii. Chance another

I discern you face to face in this float of solution. Still now,
    through my voice, you're becoming you. In tidelines,
word potions, we poets commune. From wild red and yellow light
    over the tops of houses, down into the clefts of streets,
we test truth on each other. Our lyrics swim in fear, in the
    teeth of your wolf, glazed snake, whiskered hog,
in the fly that dives to feed the hungry fingerling. Through
    the fire of half-belief, our poems are forged.

We're lending you our gaze, our questions – you asked,
    so mark them well. We're still guessing, fathoming you,
we parse you in part, beam by beam. But we're hanging on.
    There's a measure of perfection in us all, so in you also.
Say, Friend Walt, from this shadowy fold, have we light enough
    to chance another crossing? Have we courage to press
beyond our greedy rip, arrogant trip, to glide past this
    eyes-clenched drive of our own frenetic undoing?

II

Adrift

Ferry commons

On the bench hoping to pass as a chaise lounge,
     a young man rests against   the affected arm,
legs furled, warming to the Bollywood fabric, his purple Puma bag
     a tender adrift on the carpet.   He's got a tight black beard,
bright eyes. Is he a poet yet? He doesn't jot in a feathered notebook
     as I do, trying to pin tails   to a donkey's ear, sparks
to the page. Fireflies wrestle free, tack off into the understorey.

In a red swivel chair a woman drinks hard ginger beer
     bespoke-brewed in Tassie.   She prattles about
her grandchild-to-be, its sailor father who might be reeled in
     by the umbilical cord   as nothing else has,
even adult love. The young dreamer wearies of banter,
     slips off to the bar whose   cherry-plastic ceiling
mirrors whitecaps pink and disordered in our wake.

Now he's hunched over a cylinder of Pringles, tumbler of Coke,
     a straw that seems broken   but is only refracted.
Slow travel grants luxuries, a second glance, chance to relish
     delights of the ferry commons.   People-watching
seasons the swag of time weighing on us, weighing us, flock
     of amnesiacs. Months after   booking our tickets,
We're assaulted by this pause, its baffling slack.

Incantation

Here is where I long to belong, in this trough
between horizons, flanked by mindful and present,

where water sponges itself like a Welsh vale in winter.
Or is it here, on this well-swell of being, so rested

my lungs breathe bubbular out the perfect O of my mouth?
Is it floating on a lilo of ruched ripples I am fully me?

A meal of nuts, dried fruit, wriggles gently in its vessel
inside me, my vessel in this seaborne vessel, nestled

bobbing babushka dolls fixated on one port,
then, with a cardinal compass flick, avid for another.

I swim in story capsules, slip into crannies,
ride atoms that circle, cycle, pump and plot new paths

through vintage currents. Molecular schools, oxygen-
swollen, incant their one name, 'water, water, water'.

In liquid societies, borders bleed wet-on-wet,
brushes slide slick onto glazed lagoons.

Colossal diva divers teach their calves
who teach their calves furtive symphonies of the deeps,

sweet underworld echoes, molten hymns to krill
so clear, we recoil from calling this sacred thing music.

But I can't breathe between jostling cellular pods,
each droplet all its own – so little, so much for kinship.

New order

52 Pick-Up was a joke, a game they played, in a place I once
called home. I learnt how the card deck soars, smacks the ceiling,

spatters boxed on the floor – mine to crawl, peel off cold tiles, sort
in their spray of laughter. Migration's distilling, one ferry crossing

enough to toss it all in the questioning air till I'm a toddler again,
testing gravity from my high chair. Down it comes with a bump

or crash, another new order begging discernment. Maybe that's life,
I'll grow accustomed. Salt's a purge, stings the eyes of everyone

but fish. The trick through tears is to find enough gumption, wit,
an ace in the hole. A migrant clings to the thinnest hope, that going home,

forward home, I'll find a home, people to love my love. I'll embrace
a new deal, quirks of droll humour, find poise in their random order,

orthodoxies, new rules of the game. I'll know I'm home when
full of gratitude, I'm shamelessly busting to break, remake them.

Passage

Christmas wreaths with pinstripe ribbons are odd memorials
to fête a birth many call good news. Plastic-plate poinsettias

hang above portholes, daring anyone to beg prickly assistance.
Round Deck 7 passengers are wreathed, playing happy families.

How easy – a slip, a fall, chute of ten or so metres. Impact smacks,
packs a wallop, carves the surface. Some glimpse a splash,

sure at Christmas it's just a seabird. An equal plunge follows,
into ringing black where it's tough to find the top of dark.

Bass Strait isn't bitter enough for flash-freezing, flash-numbing.
Its cold's a school of minnows nibbling till the mind lapses.

A life-ring's not launched, life is a slippery proposition.
Halo-wreaths shimmy hollow cheer into the late sun.

The giving season's a magnet for high-pressure fronts.

Selfie

In urban mourning gear, staccato and animated, they picture
themselves on their phones. Screens record them at the rail,
phones mediating as life happens, instead of it happening.
Emily and Blossom, Edward and Ali, best mates for today.

> On this ferry, see us, see me. We're acting glad though beat,
> a bit green. Here I am, seeing the world. You should be green
> with envy! Mother, you recognise me! I'm invisible to others.
> The bartender shouts, says I look like I don't speak English.

The hyper-vigilant scan and scan. Digital graffiti, 'here I am'
or just 'I am' records in her phone, witnessing to herself in case
no one else does. Another airport-mall, pseudo-main street. No horror
in this eternal-return, only the soothing lull of *déjà-vu déjà*-viewed.

> I can post my shadow in a public square or inbox of a friend,
> swing up the red flag of hope at the end of her virtual drive.
> A selfie's my longing poured into a crowd, my act of resistance,
> trial balloon on the cusp of being seen, or just being.

Peace signs, Toyota jumps, show they're 'still feeling it'.
No one mentions the pain. If all the world was a stage, everyone's
a flatscreen star now. Digital existence is thin, a billboard tip.
Selfies are zero-ones, binary shadows that freelance.

> My face is the matter, pixels pinch adjustable skin, tattoo me
> into believing they're me, but their me. I'm making memories
> of a secret ache, my unconvincing life. See my digital fairy tale:
> unique, I am an alignment of variables, algorithmic art piece.

This slow poet's grasping the trigger-finger trend. The selfista's
a voyeur fixed on her days, her own memes, flip book of lols
and instant nows. I do see. With post-production edits, she's just
catching on, clutching on, to the frame, to glimmers of herself.

Sailing trapeze

The dinghy that's me sails tomato-canvased, tacks
a tight course, drum-taut, blowing free of must-do
and dusty custom. I'm racing a squall, skimming
smooth, now flying on surface tension's vacuum,
sucking me, whole flightless bird, into its void.

My feet braced on gunwales, I hold this trapeze,
swing, in balance, forty degrees to the waves – where
I'm keen to keep it. One sliver more or less spells
a hammering, bloody face bang, or frigid body dousing
and drag. Steady entails looking before and beyond.

I can't see the wind but feel its cheek on my face.
Old strands of wool stand rigid, tiny hero pennants
apart from steel stays. Zip-zapping along
in the craft of myself, today's pangs shrivel, wrinkled
fingertips turn sweet, prunes plumped into lush plums.

Unborn or dead

We've hardly touched you, moon, left a little space junk,
boot prints, flags. No relic
explains how you are to us, dawning and daunting.

It's true we're in this together, bewitched by our own
latticed tellings of you,
twining shadows of light and night, how a rock

that gathers no moss spawns quivers of lore. You can't face
another fawning poem
but not all that's lunar's been said. It takes eons to weave

a magic carpet's gasp. You are still Swiss cheese, we want
to possess you, slice you, bring you home.
You orbit a path of unatmospheric disregard. So it must be.

Leave moon-natter to us. You get on getting on.
We tangle in circles of measure
and meaning as if one night we'll have you sorted.

Hear that racket? Vulture talons screech on metal roofs,
predict death, so they say. We crave
your freelance being. Ours has the hollow of bamboo,

marrow-bone. Vultures won't come for your carcass.
You halo their scrawny necks,
football shoulders. Most of the time we're unborn or dead.

You moon, in your way, should survive,
thrive
beyond the last trace of our ravenous kind.

Lunar

Even you, far moon, must speak on my terms. Crescent means growing even when you're a cuticle waning, butter pastry

trapping golden air. You're entailed like me, looping in rings. Nothing I know, little of my ignorance escapes word games.

Your phases are named, gibbous, rotund, pumpkin harvest-huge before you are shaved light, parmesan on an al dente orbit.

I flatter you as new, fine old crone. With hardly a wobble, you host them all, meteoric visitors that glance hello

or land with fridge-emptying hungers. Gas, fire, ice pellets more ancient than suns round your revolving stage. Some dismiss you, all show,

a random dusty rock in a force that dwarfs. That's one tale. But I haven't only moon eyes. We're both elemental.

My watery cells turn to your dry, magnetic crazing. No month do you miss me, any more than a tide forgets to rise from the deep, meet its mark.

Never alone for long, in every port you find me, gauge how torn I am now. 'Go on,' you counsel, 'there's more.' Safe harbour lies within,

we know, but the course to reach it rides the longest rollers. Your borrowed glow floods my nights, shouts me rounds of hope.

Light without dark's not much to see, dark alone can't be spoken. Dimming too you lift, stretch out your blue *boro* quilt, faded relic

that landscapes me warm, drowsy, wrapt in your dapples. Your streamers on loan fleece curly, moon-down rounding my nest of sleep.

The octopus's mending

No help in the jade of seasick faces, I go aloft alone for a spot of mending.
    It's simple, like inviting a freewheeling button to rejoin its coat.
Paddock-sized sails can't wait for the balm of anchorage. I climb
    the ratlines, leap the gulch onto the yardarm. Hand over hand
slides me into cloud-jam, the airy theatre of operation. Here I must
    forget the golden rule, 'Keep one hand for you, one for the ship.'

Perched on this pivot, fix your eyes and stomach on the seesaw horizon.
    Lean forward, balance your ribs on the yard, appendages
serve as ballast, but not only. Don't look down. Clean the wounds,
    draw gaping sides together. Rough tacks offer first aid.
Knot tied, thread snipped, slip the tail through the eye. Repeat.

Cold fingers fumble. If you drop a needle, don't look down, it's deep
    in yesterday's sea, why a knife on its lanyard never parts from
your belt. Double stitching will hold as much forever as is given a sail.
    Sliced from swatches, grafts promote healing. Keep sutures fine,
take time. Scars remind us, this too will pass. Don't look down or back.

Scorched by rain's lashing, at last I regain the mast. My mind aslosh,
    body memory pretzels me for descent. One leg round the stay,
the other locks over, upturned toe braces against shroud. Taking flight
    from this billowy sky I swoop, one wing outstretched, down
to the tipsy deck, to retrieve a dull pulse for polishing acres of brass.
    They say rainy day mending's so soothing.

Reunion

I hold my breath on board, stuck on the in
of salt-fragrant air, the out of letting go.
But diesel fumes reek industry, four engines,

a cosmic monster, this transpiring body ploughs
water as a hot snowplow tackles a car park under
a heavy fall. As if it is still snowing, it pushes,

growls and spits. Like the Red Sea parting, the strait
closes over the moment we pass. Planing's efficient,
hovering electric, a giant hummingbird hulk.

Yet to float my own water body's more stirring,
not flailed by stabilisers that sever the ear's
good sense. On my back I'm one vast elastic skin.

My ribs pump in tune with the rise and fall, crest
and trough, our one seething chest. Reunion.
My face surges up to the scudding sky, oval cut-out,

joker at a fairground. Don't mention carousels
or fairy floss. Afternoon oodles will sigh me along,
all my tickets on crests of heaving contentment.

Piñada

Vessels can't wait for kind winds
when the world keeps wanting.
To reach Aden, Montréal, Rio
or Freo is always urgent.

A small vessel in high seas
rears and plunges, porpoising. Crew
make fast, repair, haul in or loose
lines against hurtling forces.

I breathe on the up, brace
for a sluicing when the bowsprit
skewers a crest's green guts.
But one emphatic swell sweeps me

    overboard –

    Here, here is a new time zone
    on my safety line, hanging
    against the hull I'm cold, covert,
    a clapper without a bell,

    knuckles knocking at a steely door,
    tethered party piñada
    wacked soggy, spilling
    not lollies but sweeter prayer

    until later, much later –

I'm hauled up, gill-less fish sputtering,
meat-mallet depleted, tenderised, they call it.
Oddly victorious, I smile between shivers
at the frayed end of a grey cotton rope.

Double-ender

This craft of me is no grand liner,
double-ender rowboat more like.
Beamy, my ribs are bumpers deflated,

a slap of varnish more than
all the make-up I can bear. A plastic bailer's
handy on a line, might do as a sunhat,

but brings small solace to blisters,
brine-pickled feet and heart. Though squelchy,
sand shoes do quack glad as ducks

in a downpour. I'm glad too
for life preservers, my own flotation, recalling
'chin-up' is my only blowhole.

My rowlocks creak and loosen, release
sweeps of salt-shame. Face-up I can
pull through it all, meet halcyon waters.

My keel's brighter than lead sounds,
calm umpire between torque and twist,
relentless tussle of lee and windward.

Perhaps being born a gemini, two-spirited,
I see two sides to any wave,
one that lifts and carries, one that burnishes.

III

Into Port

The shallows

Tidal flats form a parallel world, jam-packed with liminal,
both and neither-nor. Who are you, slipping on this sliver?
Don't just watch, let loose the natter tickling your tongue
to the white-fronted chat, to pebbles that mud-mutter.

If you see red freckles on smooth-spotted crabs, your paws
or flukes are awash in the halfway. Briny ones may petrify
if you fluster, spread your whimbrel wings. Be gentle
raising your needle-beak, curlew's arc, double-edged,

weapon and art piece. This zone's tight with the slosh
of life. Crabs are already sharing your thoughts with hula fish,
swirly turban shells are glossing about being swaddled,
velvet seaweed's gossiping on to the shy beaded glasswort.

It's not our hold on the green shelf of self, but our own
sublime liquid life we have othered. Every home swills
and swallows. We fear our own salt tears, spilt milk
and blood's dark drops, cringing in the wet crotch of sorrows.

Swimmer, don't apologise. Better grow real, unashamed
of your hydrous self, see the moon as your true compass.
Who will cry for us, confused like sea dragons
at Mardi Gras, when soon or sooner rising tides claim us?

On the verge

And so we come. Come back
to earth. Projected from the nose
of a ferry into the viral verge

of the decade, we enter this world
unswaddled, not speaking
its new languages of risk and fear.

Our once-secluded shore metes out
a fast-sheering sanctuary.
Storm's whip has come to meet us,

its tail stings in the breach.
The tarmac's slick with leaves, twigs,
nettled olive branches,

frond litter flying from
gums, not ticker tape at all, but a pall
where bitter shadows lengthen.

Ordinary miracles

Ferry-riding's a bittersweet communion,
together, side-by-side, devouring banquets
of one sort and another. This vessel's just a cup
on the water, scheduled in trust to carry us,
our cars, precious claptrap to the next
chance bead, story to tell in our rosary lives.
A boarding pass is a ticket to hear – his fear,
her truth, their hope – lapping against our
erosion-proofed shores. Don't borrow trouble,
some say. But how are open-air confessionals
sealed? It's easy to dismiss crossing, gentle
binding through idle hours of spectacle,
infomercial, product placement. Having earned
a pass from Sniffy, the quarantine dog,
will I recall this day crowded with raw truths,
ordinary miracles? Thanksgiving needs no
consecration, it's the blessing of knowing
we're blessed. In this tossed passenger-salad,
fluke of our Aussie calendar, holy days,
or at least holidays, offer snippets of sanctity.

First

Dishevelled old man, loafing.
Luckless beard, jumper fish-oil caked.
Great Southern Ocean flotsam.

Boozy night? Hadley's Orient Hotel
may be selective about smell.
He smells it now, victory sweet,

not luck, but calculation steeped
in musk, Arctic campfires, sharp
expert lessons on coldest living.

That music of dogs straining before
the sled, bright breath, waxed skis
whistling, shhh-shhh, shhh-shhh,

rhythm slicing powder. Now *Fram*'s
a quaint harbour miniature,
scrimshaw tethered to quicksilver.

Sixteen huskies howl on her deck,
frustrate Hobart dog catchers.
First light, the man, bathed younger,

appears at the post office door. Last time
'in the public interest' they stole
his news. Now coded telegraphs fly

to Norway. Damn the English, there's
ice enough and more for all.
But the pole, delicious pole, is ours.

Roald Amundsen (b. Norway, 1872) reached the South Pole on 14 December 1911 and sent news of the achievement from Hobart Post Office on 7 March 1912. Amundsen successfully navigated the Northwest Passage 1903–06. He disappeared in June 1925 on an Arctic rescue flight.

No return

In the Isle of Man

Ramsey Harbour's a mud belly drained of current,
ocean sapped out beyond the pier. Half the fleet's at sea,
no popping home for a cuppa or chips and gravy, pie
with mushy peas till the tide ekes in. Down quay walls,
other vessels hang slack on lines, lobster pots stacked tight,
keels squat in the ooze, exposing paunches starved of paint.

Gulls, terns and plovers, the odd swan, oyster-catchers
paddle in the slippy shallows, catching algae, tiny fish,
molluscs or krill that burrow into slurp twice each day.
Pub goers, café-ballast perch their matchbox cars
on the lip above, display proud cardboard play-clocks.
'No return' isn't a lament for the perils of sea

but a rule of the parking game. Referees pass at least twice
annually. Locals translate for me, 'Don't adjust your clock
once it's set.' And '*Rheynn Arragh*' disappointingly doesn't
mean 'rein in your raft' but 'Department of Transport'.
Ramsey folk, raised at the mouth of the 'wild garlic river'
couldn't stomach any trade in lieu of ancient tidal rhythms.

Thirteen miles away, half an island, now Peel's got it all,
they say – marina humming round the clock, castle built
by Saint Patrick on holiday, a Viking museum and crests
of the island's best, Davison's Whippy – in cup or cone.
Over in Peel too, seals play nosey in the bay, warm their fins
in soft rain, and eider ducks return at any hour they please.

The end of the road

Idling in Southport, we drift up to the Rocket Café.
It's a plastic water tank with nautical lights, controls.

We sniff lavender soap, buy mugs of milky 'house' chai.
Frogs preach to the black going-nowhere rivulet

reflecting a canopy of peach and pewter limbs.
We plunk down on hessian stools, steady pottery mugs

on a silvering crate. I'm leafing through sad poetry
from an elated circus tent, the Little Free Library moored

to an opposite post. Bitzer-pups lead full-grown men
who wonder aloud if they know us. A woman observes

our red-brim hats, cherry-framed glasses. Snap! Strangers
are a big event at the end of the road. From the counter,

locals sip water, shoulder-check us often, to be sure.
They ponder again if they've seen the back of frost,

when to dig in tomatoes. Last outpost before the Antarctic,
this hamlet's cautious under psychedelic night skies.

Most feel only lukewarm about possible space adventure,
wary even of this romp and shudder we call spring.

One stroke

At that improbable moment
when the disk has slipped
behind buttery hills
or those hills have pooled
to eclipse the glint of dish,
when the river's more alive
than the dilute-pastel sky

just then. Just then
the pair comes

surface and dive
surface and dive,

unfeasible, gymnasts looping
through this glazed plane.

Curve of dorsal, comb of spine
part a thin black line
spinning upriver,
across an orange-marbled page –
soft-leaded pencil trailing
its humble underline
to close this day.

Never mind I'm fourteen

Andy's lashes are gorgeous, never mind I'm fourteen,
no excuse for how sexy I find him, tousled by the night.

>He leaps back on board, steadies, spews over my sand shoes.
>It's what sailors, real men, learn to do. Only the guy

who pays shows ID in a bottle shop. Stroking his wad
of change, he leaves youth to grog up in a parking lot.

>They'll be shipboard by dawn, not to get caught,
>left in port, soused and under age. Never mind

I'm fourteen, I see the flash on his jaw, lipstick – oh –
or tomato sauce for chips now spattered, worming pink

>over my feet? Andy's off his face, never mind
>the job I've got getting him down the hatch,

big bag of spuds. After, he only ever looks through me.
We call it growing up. Officers, at sixteen or seventeen,

>take shore leave in baggy borrowed whites.
>Men-in-training leave women-in-training to scrub

mess off the decks, give the brass a Brasso massage.
A girl learns early, home and away, every shame is hers –

>just cope, just hide, just disappear dirty jobs,
>make men's world clean and fresh. At eight bells

the ship's Master rises, wants his usual, runny yolks,
hash browns, glossy mound of limp bacon. But phew,

>he's humming, not hot-mad but deaf to night thuds,
>splutters. Thickly rust-bearded at twenty-nine,

he holds sway. He's learnt to expect, and so to stir
miracles, his messes all to be vanished.

Finian's call

In sixth-century Ireland, two Saint Finians made their mark.

At Kerry's Chioll I set my load. Slats that bend, skins, thongs, fat to seal.
The young poke and tease at my oddments. 'Where to, this *curach*, Abba?

Won't be far!' 'We go with the Spirit,' I invite. Perils thrill, hands busy.
I feel already her cradle. 'Who will sail with blind-leper Finian?' I ask.

There are murmurs. 'Then go, sup. If blessing is given, return.
The tide is fair.' In the cool, I hear steps. My hands open to see each.

Several muscular, big, one slender-fingered, a musician, one is soft like
a priest. Another's fine-boned like a fish, calloused – a boy? No, a woman,

cara. She'll carry her secret as long she can. Not the vessel but some
higher power calls. Brawny lads evade their herds, I'm no one

to judge a leading. Some know the arts of stone. We're enough.
We stow our seeds, roots, tools and loaves, cast off in laughter's splash.

'Who brings gifts of steering? Who of paddling?' 'Make for that fin,
crag Sceilg Mhichal.' Late, our isle approaches. Eerie voices, shearwaters

chant where they burrow and lay. The *curach*'s wild, a bucking calf eluding
rock's froth. Under the big moon a tiny harbour opens. I'm lifted to a ledge.

'Abba, Abba, what comes first?' 'Haul our craft higher?' 'Make shelter?'
'Breathe, friends. Love is our one refuge. Lay your palms on your mother.'

'Rest your forehead in her warmth, thank her for your sweet delivery.'
No mind now for soaked garments, *leine* and *brat*, cowls that slap us

with wet-sheep smell. Flames ticktack, twig to grass to driftwood.
Limbs twine eager into sleep's heat. Tomorrow we'll lay the first stones

of our hive. I'm only a midwife. But I dream we stay a thousand present
gifted years, sipping slowly round and round the cup of this horizon.

On the charts

In this wood-scented cabin, I practise navigation,
    'dead-reckoning', tacking wildly from mind to charts.

    Poems are scrawled not on legends but the bluest bits,
        fathoming open seas, nosing round for deep harbours.

I'm striving for light through chewed pencils, dirty weather.
    There are rules to be broken – correct for compass error,

    triangulate, maths I forgot before learning make me seasick.
    Better I take life on the currents, tides as boons.

I sail on rhythms, knack and nose, slippery shanties, some that
    get away, a bonzer that stays to warble.

    The best haven can shield, just on the dot, or be dazzling,
        curled into the sheltering hook of a question mark.

Anybody's god

Pyres burn day and night on the Ganges. At dawn grass brooms
tickle ash to the lip, freeing spirits
to ride holy waters out beyond the virus. Woodcutters might relish

this festival fever if their stick-legs did not have so far to walk,
forests shrinking, distancing by the hour
from Varanasi's sacred shores. With half an eye for buses,

cows, pilgrims, fuel foragers snooze pushing sway-axle carts,
bald tyres stuffed with plastic bags.
None of us holds air for the long haul. There's no profit cremating

bodies dumped by families who can't afford another death.
This holy city's kind, upstream they send
their turmericked mummies swathed in half-bleached saris.

Plastic flower necklaces float the distance vivid. Soon the dead come
dressed as they sickened, fat as if feasting
were their last act. The news reports new viral business beyond

online shopping. In Peru's dark, grave-robbers stack bodies in plots
dug by others who sweated naive
in blind-hot morning grief. Now the sick dig-their-own in fevers,

fall frazzled into these furrows, gasping, begging anybody's god
for cover, a good simple dusting.
Stench defies words, but our bodies soon pass beyond nose, smell,

beyond mantra, beyond even the breezy Oom of broom grass.

IV

Excursion

Centrifugal

Like sails solar panels stand angled on Colorbond,
creaking hope through corrugate, pumping our immodest lives.

Sun turbines never luff but stir unseen, packing wires with tension,
punch that dribbles, wriggles, bubbles out to all the world.

But what of this boisterous wind? Will its bluster fly me
sulphur-crested, cockatooing, crown to leafy crown?

Will it cut me down, a fractured sparrow scrabbling seeds
that chooks distain? Wind summons keys of winding spheres,

whirling galaxy tails. Let's plant a spinning daisy garden,
pinwheel chorus, turbines in bumble-humming unison.

Our smug suburbs bristle with aerials, chimneys, steeples
to Jenga games of profit and loss. Flashing headlights, floodlights

wash out our stars. Let windflowers spin to sweeten our fears,
jazz up the day, slow-waltz the gloaming of climate nightfall.

A thousand miles from care

Call me ferry fan, ferry-phile, ferry fiend, no name captures
the simple pleasures of these more-ish gliders, tangy-textured

crowds, mosaics of colour, culture, crunch, wild meets tame,
trying finds true. No ferry sails without torque of surprise,

engine's sudden puff and rev, mad mingling scents, cumin meets
fish meets diesel, raw edges, the known's startled skin turning

inside out. In petrified runnels they ply their tick-tack,
Circular Quay to Manly's surf, Dover to Calais.

On Istanbul's Bosphorus ferries crisscross to Kadikoy, Karakoy,
even Harem. By ferry odd cities are twinned, Osaka to Shanghai,

yin-yang-yin, forty-five hours of moon to sun and moon again.
Some ferries transgress, infringe. Helsinki to Tallinn, West Block

to East, spelled bargain-shopping for Finns, but greater hope
sailed west to test for asylum. Vancouver to Victoria, a Leviathan

slips between rock and rockier, steals my breath.
The snorting camel caravan melts through a needle, into Odin's

single eye. Staten Island Ferry's tied, best bargain and treat.
A quarter's a song for Manhattan's lights, to kiss the toes

of Liberty, bless Ellis Island, all the souls who didn't make it.
But I hear now that crossing is free. No price fits a ticket to awe.

Brimming vessels

A monk clutches his glinting load to his chest more closely
        than day-trippers tote trays of coffee,
gooey iced-slice, even big-bummed babies bumping along
        on shoulders. In the ship's café,
Laminex tables are territories colonised for forty minutes.
        Fifteen bearded men, despite tattoos,

are not pirates, but stake possession with frizzy infants.
        Everyone's got a holiday from power suits
and uniforms. Four ages of Sri Lankan women drape their folds
        on plastic chairs. Their sportswear
billboard-men say yes to Optus, Chemist's Warehouse,
        cheers to a pending cricket tragics' picnic.

Pre-dawn the jaunty monk woke to polish his super-sized alms bowl.
        They say in the West
a gaping great bowl is a must to press the rite of alms. It's not about
        begging and having but
giving and letting go. Sparking online lives of detachment,
        the monk types smartly with both thumbs

into his iPhone. Attention to now is the one pursuit, tomorrow's bounties
        are only hazards till safely left behind,
and even then. Try to sail clear of expectation's highs, windfalls that gleam
        in shiny-toothed shoals off your bow.

Sydney experiments

By breach Sydney ferries were born, some proving seaworthy
for a bit. Curious folk, curiouser craft plied the womb of 'ocker Aus'.
In Port Jackson, crossing like living meant risk, but any price
bettered overland bumps, ruts and ooze. Even for the governor,

ferryman Billy Blue told a crack Jamaican tale, convict tricks
up his commodore sleeves. 'Rescued' rum barrels splashed, lashed
to his dwarfish craft. His ballads paced his rowing, so a cove
on a job got a real fair go, sleight of hand, slice of time to melt

out of sight. The oddest of ferries was one brazen *Experiment*,
fetching up at Parramatta in four hours unless she drifted
for the Heads. Passengers were lost in chess, or raucous round
the plinkety piano, tripping on sun, cheap grog. Four horses,

apocalyptic, carouselled round the deck, churning the capstan,
paddle wheel, skiving off in swelters or southerlies. With a slip
of ship-shippery, *Experiment* took a boiler, whitewashed her wiles,
rebirthed a new novice slicing Brisbane's brackish floes.

Manly Ferry, 1939

For Patricia Firkin

The crisp-braided girl from Kurri Kurri knows
      the tang of shame, coal silt crusting dusty
          on schoolyard, laundry, mother's moods.

Manly ferry's an elixir, promised ribbon of bliss,
      a 'holiday' – city name for delight. But this
          Sydney noon is dark and sleety, upsy-tummy.

Steely walls, hulls, guns, the ferry slinks sheepish
      beneath ciphers all tugging toward code-word 'Europe'.
          Sharp-nosed ships glower at chipper ferries.

The uncles mutter, voices tight in case the girl,
      chin propped on rail, has ears for the leaden weight of it.
          Her cry falls wide and silent: don't they see, spring's

grey pall's a warning, colour's forfeit a clue? Cold grips
      her neck, this Manly spree's a hoax sinking under lies.
          Coming days will cut, her words for 'torn' mound up:

casualty, amputee, refugee, shell-shock has none
      of shelly beaches' awe. Her toes will poke worm-mauve
          from criss-cross sandals – no more shoes for sprouts.

Only boots stomp-stomp aboard, away.
      Battle leaves children to grieve alone the soft and
          nameless thing they've lost, war's truth ajar.

Isle of Man Caravan Club

This is the big weekend, the kipper barbecue. We wait all year for this. Some come fifteen miles. At the Point of Eyre, the vans face Scotland, keep an eye out. It's how we've always done it. The grass is a golf green, thanks to sheep. Or wallabies. They escaped the wildlife sanctuary. Or wind may not allow for grass.

That lighthouse towers like a factory chimney. Currents run strong. George's dog drowned retrieving a ball. It was a tern confused Butternut. Most unkind. In the sixties I think. Our waters toss boulders like hay bales. We don't go on the beach, perfect spot to twist an ankle. These waters used to teem with kippers, well, Manx mackerel. I don't know now.

Mary gets the kippers, she's secretary. Arthur does the barbecue, his is the biggest. Got a smart red awning. Won't stand up to wind though, he's had it repaired four times, they see him coming. We camp at the point Friday, to be there for the big day. Always lots of beer, though more tea gets drunk in the end. Funny how it works out. Mostly we're inside, it's that wet. We go calling van to van, steaming up with chatter, it's lovely. Maeve doesn't allow boots in her van.

We come six miles, worth it unless we meet oncoming. Reversing's the thing. One looks forward, the other back, if we're tired we make do with the video. Ah, that smell, kippers, twice smoked, crisping in their skins, would bring hundreds. But the prevailing's in the wrong direction, so thirty vans get out. If they miss, they're poorly.

Some don't have vans any more. They keep up their membership, nothing stops them coming for kippers. Last camp of summer. Can hardly call it that, shocking weather. One year we had a good month. Which was it, dear? Well, the kippers are a stand-out. Summer isn't what it was. Going to the shore with cousins, you wouldn't now. Winters we fly to the Canaries for a breath of sea air.

Lessons from the Bellevue

I've blown through many lives, leaping in early, wriggling round
as I did at the derelict Bellevue Hotel. Its doors blew free, blizzards danced
in the lounge with puffs of kapok, horsehair, mouse droppings.

> Mum recalled tea on the veranda, wild blueberry pie picked
> and baked flakey by Edna, Ojibwe woman, kitchen helper. At the other end
> of her big life, I loved her salt-and-pepper hair, great fisher queen.

Her few words, silken silence. Her red amoebic cardigan, leaky
wooden boat, dodgy outboard engine that roared, naked,
cover long gone. How Edna could laugh to include you and the lake.

> Just a summer resident, I rambled round borrowing as we did
> at home, clean undies, matching earrings, a chewed Bic pen. In our white
> fibreglass runabout I rescued a hotel chair, not knowing theft.

Ah, the aura that protects some kids. I painted it blue with a tin I found
alongside kerosine, in our old dunny. Late I learnt not to hold
my breath at raw smells, tight places, the rule of do least harm.

> That Bellevue Hotel, old wooden palace condemned, never did burn
> beyond my imagination. I still see holes where winter ice tore
> red tiles off the roof. Other lessons from the sturdy guest house,

fortify to windward, keep your tears for sunsets, nothing,
including you, is quite what it seems. And push off hard,
let go early, jetties leave you rich with splinters and ghosts.

Barging in

The Tarkine World Heritage Area of north-west Tasmania is an Aboriginal Cultural Landscape. It includes buttongrass plains, many rare or endangered species, and Australia's biggest remaining temperate rainforest.

Fatman barge crawls crabby, side-on, grooving
    across the slick glass seal, ceiling over
    the Pieman River's bottomless canyon.

A raft of a ferry, damselfly wings for ramps,
    it clutches its oracle, old cable, rusty vine
    known to yield in spring floods.

Without this ferry, the ravelled thread that ties
    Zeehan to Smithton, Smithton to Zeehan,
    would melt mossy into rainforest profusion.

Then where would we be? Fatman's the living link
    in this gravel-spool, back-of-the-drawer
    kitchen string, no real highway to the world.

Inky to the verge, our Pieman River gapes
    at the Great Southern Ocean,
    biblical walls of water pounding in from Africa.

On its bank squats Corinna, loose excuse for a village
    where bread was scant but gold held out
    for a month or two, long enough to bring them in.

Those wannabe ghosts – clawed scratchers, shifty sievers,
    slouching button-eyed corpses, digging, digging,
    through snow, even by lamp in the dark.

Corinna's pub oiled these parts, rebirthing the wild west.
    Even now they roll in, float across.
    Jeeps, campervans, Hiaces, lured by remote corrugate.

There's plenty here – dust, rust on rust, two residents,
    a ferryman ready to cross
        on the strength of a cooee or matey wave.

It's takayna, our Tarkine, whose lungs you hear expand.
    Decay's display, tannin's tea waters
        reflect bright the limelight of their verdant sisters.

Like abalone in a silk kimono, lustre dazzles from folds.
    Dense with wilder-wonder,
        myrtle and leatherwood honey the sky.

Recall

This river's a balm of indulgence – I'm at the helm
of *Arcadia* on the Pieman River, sleek antique,

Art Nouveau benches from Hobart's next-to-last trams.
The antediluvian engine – before Hydro dammed the river –

is frenzied, overheating. The two young crew slipped
down the hold some time ago. Can I land this load of tourists,

this vessel too long avoiding a Cape Grim transit
for an overhaul in Burnie? We're that bloody-minded here.

Until she catches fire, tourists vanish leaving cash, or there's
a click, dead silence when they come to warm her, there'll

be packed lunches, languid day excursions with names
like 'Sweetwater', a chance at the helm, fingers crossed.

Will she weather wild seas under tow, engine dead cold?
Ah Tassie, it mostly all works out on a wing and prayer, or two.

Begging buckets

In Burkina Faso, West Africa

I was heartless, took them for granted before revelation – a running tap's
    sweeter than dawn's call to prayer. Pilgrims come early to late
clanking jerry-built buckets, kerosine tins, cooking oil drums,
    hammered, rolled, and leaky-as. Balanced, these crowning vessels

slice forehead scars on the home trek. Their brave-necked, laden bearers
    may sing loudest. Revolution decrees water gush
for those who pay, no ear for hand-to-mouth, parched tongues, the warble
    of living reeds. My spigot burbles for my white skin,

innocent to thirst's rage, pliant to my lucky lotto ticket some call development.
    Hallowed portal, this tap seals my privilege, here where we all quaff
Saharan sand, itch its salt from our creases. Even rest's not freely given.
    Each breath swelters. I curl on my plastic mat, drinking moonlight

with parties of squalling mosquitos. I'm finely netted, not promising quarry.
    My tap's a shrine, reels in faithful from this back-of-the-train-station
quarter. They come from our market's sweaty swarm no tourist sees
    – socket-eyed thong-repair boys, skeletal tomato girls

in riotous prints, open-air butchers whose best patrons are flies
    at an all-they-can-eat buffet. Like any temple mine strikes awe:
its red gate cowers behind a totem beached on its axles,
    rusty oil tanker squatting smug and smugger with years.

We're all just flowing through, glistening, Old-Testament tumbled.
    What are specks in a shimmering savannah? Here living's
a bloodsport that desiccates at speed. But one pale amulet clinches refuge,
    a clear flow, slopping enchantment into my begging bucket.

V

Rough Passage

Laws of the sea

This stretch of deck's loud with live broadcasting.
A self-amplifying woman doesn't snoop

in her daughters' rooms for fear of something
thrown at her. But she knows Beth keeps a bulging

stash of jellybeans, sour cherry, expresso, key lime,
sometimes double fudge, under her bed, they're a bit

hard to reach. It's nothing personal, she just doesn't
want her girls going through what she has.

The ship police enforce Laws of the Sea, ridding us
of crime, vociferous noise, bare feet on coffee tables.

A deckhand informs us reclining's not on. They know
an inside cabin's too dear for a day crossing. Who pays

to be the ham in a bunk-sandwich, far from caffeine,
TV, pokies, where you might at least win between losses?

A bursar posts bylaws: 'One: Medicate before you feel sick.
Two: Assume a prone position' (reclining's illegal,

but point your chin up, head back, think of England).
We may come to hate the terms, but reckoned as a comma,

required punctuation, we hold on. Some may even
sing along to the rough ruffles, jounce of this crossing.

Corked

Sailing broadside in the Roaring Forties,
even a ten-storey ferry's a cork. Towering clouds

have nothing on these tumbling castles
menacing our tiny toys, cars, dogs and ponies

in the hold. Creamy Tassie cheeses snuggle down
to rock and roll in refrigerated trucks.

A blink of time makes so much clearer:
what are friends, love's reductions, shimmering

before brute force polishes us again with
detonating wash. Being a cork recalls what matters

when holidays distort with sandy fables – goodness
traps enough air to rise above the glib and gritty.

In this vessel, wild ocean wiles slap and roll
like an old-time pub after six o'clock swill.

Bull waves hurl at each other, no mind for corks.
This ferry's my vat, my ferment I cling to, even

cherish its homely disorder. The sublime is easy
on the eyes, hard on a walnut-mind struggling

with sky and sea, slippery horizon, a squiggle
drawn in the middle distance by a fine grey pen.

Terminus

In the warp of ferry-time, my mind shuttles forward and back
to questions of momentum. Transit has its interchanges, snarls.
I hone in on the edginess of buses, their amphibious limits
when shifting a town, its bars, pokies, shops, public toilets.

Even a sticky-floored cinema, parking-tower gloom and twin
peak idling-hours are embraced in this ferry's vibe. Bus tickets
are cheap, but ride-sharing dangles intimate chats I too often
miss in a crowd. It's the volley of seat-back banter, time

to admire the curve of a head, translucent lip of ear in late sun,
joining the gravitas glibly called 'neck'. I recall bus terminals.
Toronto's wrought-iron mezzanine was smoky, a ship's rail
in pea-soup fog. Through a New York night I straggled round,

marooned in the Port Authority – the last Jersey bus had sailed.
Everyone else knows it's part bus station, part marrow-chilling
wind tunnel, where it pays to chum up to gangs for company.
Tullamarine's bus mall echoes nautical in its mixed-up diesel pride.

One can jump off early, avoid finalities, the grief of terminus –
advice not serving me well afloat. I might adopt '*ne regrette rien*',
good counsel for bus-riders in particular. But mid-Bass Strait,
it's high time to flex, accept the crunchy with the smooth.

Sorry to have missed you

Dear Gran, it doesn't matter you couldn't cook. I want to say
how your loves sparked and caught. Mills & Boons
made good kindling. We cleared the shed, scorched scores

of bottomless kettles. You always fancied a 'wee cuppa', an arrowroot
from the biscuit museum on the bench.
But your words slid away till only 'the aspect, the aspect' was left,

plump fingers grasping at air. I'm sorry you didn't know my name,
have your own, not even 'architect', so hard won.
Lost in your drawer of drawers, among grey shapeless bloomers

lay your gold medal. Genius, fully rigged in you was a grand
barque caught in a cough-mixture bottle.
Babe-in-arms on the *Aurania*, you swept wife-washed into dry dock.

Then, keeping watch on suburbia, you waited, waited for your
'ship to come in'. By the brimming Swedish ashtray,
smoking, hazy years cocooned you in that liver-mohair cardigan.

Too late, I'm proud of you, your resilient Jewish skin. I see how
living with him, forced to 'pass',
you shrivelled. I never knew your falling gardens, floating houses,

modern-wondrous designs, perched before their time on filmy
blueprint hillsides. I'm so sorry I missed you.
But your eyes tug in me still. Now at last I am poetry's province.

Flags of convenience

As we sail south, cross the wake of Sorrento's ferry, little gull,
    we pass Portsea, a too-double name, whose milling
turquoise waters quiz what grieves us. It's not the post-Christmas
    adieu, though no circle recurs. Not the embrace or spurning

of homemade gifts given with equal heart, not even the forgotten
    brandy butter, or trials of this bushfire smoke-haze.
We're passing salt-caramel beaches, sand cliffs, the ocean faces
    of Mornington. Most shoals we mask with food, drink,

flags of convenience while pain throbs. We slice the rip between heads,
    the double tails of Melbourne. I call the lie lonely, but other
names are as apt: hungry, shamed, scared. One stooped great-auntie
    squashes a souvenir cap into her black-petalled hold-all.

What is it that makes a thing funereal, venereal? The shop's
    'Tasty Cheese Salad and Fruit Chutney Classic Sandwich' is
a big mouthful, thin shroud for her losses. Auntie tells strangers
    she's never had a holiday, her truckie husband, bless him,

hated holidays. We all have a thousand faces, ways to say I love
    Pears soap, its amber translucence, but its scent's too carnal,
familiar, wrong. Sometimes nobody's in the home strait, just
    a stale drift of motes as blinds snap, recoil, and tassels taunt.

Reading room exclusive

Here in the Reading Room, a stretch of Deck 7 with a name.
It's seven hours since Station Pier's peeling paint that gave

boatloads of migrants a flaky welcome, seven hours
since we fled the cruise ship that shabbied our ferry.

We two companions share Woolf's *A Room of One's Own*,
whisper-reading to the other a water-warped copy lent new

by a friend. What would Virginia make of this 'Reading Room',
its logo, back-to-back Rs like Playboy bunnies, accenting

alliteration we already caught? A fledgling woman in a black
Exclusively Me T-shirt bruises her lips with purple sugar-ice

emerging phallic from a cylinder. The Quiet Police are reading
their Riot Act to a mother carrying on about family to family

and the rest of us. Virginia too carries on. Fiction, she claims,
is best suited to women's narrow, parlour-framed existence.

I'm almost envious. What would she make of a BYO readery,
wallpaper figured with blank spines, no shelves, no pages?

Titles can rock anyone's boat. As modern diners must be
content with the menu, postmodern she-warriors source titles

from Amazon. Is meaning now just a fill-in-the-blanks game?
Exclusive Girl's fussing about ironing tomorrow's uniform,

being exclusively her is a weekend venture. Virginia fears
female minds aren't free for poetry, fed only on the dust of tasks.

Our literary mothers hardly got a taste for the sea, even
the expanding measure of ten hours on a ferry. They couldn't

dream of how Exclusive Girl would progress her gender, licking
nutty ice cream, bling-robed in vacuum-metallised plastic.

People of the ferry

MS *Superfast III* (serving Patras, Greece to Ancona, Italy) sustained an electrical fire in 1998. In a truck on a vehicle deck, fourteen Kurdish migrants died of smoke inhalation. In 2002 TT Lines purchased the ship, renamed *Spirit of Tasmania II*, to serve the Melbourne to Devonport crossing.

i. Royar (where the sun rises)

Royar stretches, toes push against something,
someone, soft comfort.
Neither pulls away. The canvas of sleep tugs,
persistent child.

Later, a tickle, gasp, his chest's exploding.
Smoke! Shouts,
pounding, hurtling shoulders, thud, thud within
the van's sour belly.
Bolts hold firm. Royar furls numb into himself.

Gran's beehive breads are wafting – oh, burning?
Run, Royar, run!
His chest has no puff, legs, grown small, are stony.
These auric loaves,
honeyed food of Allah, some days are all the manna
heaven and earth can muster.

ii. Helin (bird's nest, sun ray)

Helin will not play in loamy grass under the olive's
blue cloud. She will not know the lap

of her spoilt cat at its milk, the marmalade silk coat
curled in her lap, shimmering that gold of vines amid

purple hills, the bright autumn breath of Tuscany.
Helin won't know Royar's father-hands, musical

fingers clapping loudest at her grad, his black crown
streaked suave with waves of survival. Helin,

last child, a charm, vote of faith in this new life,
will not be born here. Courage brought him to try,

try again, to flee so his children could grow safe,
see Father a proud farm picker, surgeon's hands

calloused, cracked so they flourish in a land where
rubble, guns, rape are not daily fare or even likely,

where a morning stroll to school on a fresh-scrubbed
footpath holds the potent gleam, luxury of boredom.

But there's nothing grand in slicks of human filth,
in sweaty palms, raw throat, the burn of greedy smoke.

In the hold of this truck in this ship, Royar choked.
The driver chose his own skin, left his Kurds for cargo

in the van – like a used coffee cup rolling, soiling
the cab floor, fending for itself. Helin will not be born.

iii. You

If you've nothing to mull in this
    hammock of a day swinging easy
        between Monday and Wednesday,
            spare a thought for smoke

as it billows, sneaks through cracks,
    for fourteen of us – people – stuck
        in a truck in the hold of this hold.
            Our lives were retrenched,

no name, no name worth knowing,
    not name-worthy? Or was each
        of us a perfect gift
            of grace, of breath and bone?

When truth's loose, cut adrift, will you reel it home?

Submariner

In support group Jonah strokes his salty beard,
human periscope in his hoodie. This midlife
landfall assails. Too long sheltered from
surface tensions, his defences lie down deep.

Submariners in their bullet homes live
bell-to-bell, six-hour watch to six-hour watch,
work-study-work-sleep, oxygen-deprived.
Engines thrum, hatches clang, forced air stales.

A reed snorkel sips the breeze, siphons it down.
But wake steady as a pelican's draws raptors.
Satellites, like gods' eyes, circle. Jonah loves
her to dissection, gauges, compression tanks,

valve thrusters, each oily anatomical intimacy.
Sardined in bunks three high, vinyl curtains hide
wasted desire, nails bitten to the bloody quick,
flirtations with self-harm – not to risk discharge.

Fat pay cheques don't get spent undersea.
On perennial shore leave now, Jonah craves
a pod devoid of glare, of shifting light,
a fortified home where colours don't hurt.

Old submariners fish for numbness in grog
or harder. Marriages are castaway driftwood,
weekends with the kids hard work. They do like
TVs night watch, sleeping till three of an arvo.

It's mates Jonah misses, scattered down the coast,
glued to the edge. He dozes by day, nights
cruises ebay for Special Forces gear on Afterpay,
expensive excuse for bobble-head yarning.

From limpet-life below the rip, adrenalin-weary,
Jonah's caught in a diluted backwater of pulse.
All vivid dreams of shore leave, the provocations
of life submerged, even its obliteration, elude.

The lure

I clutch my boarding pass, folder rigid with warnings,
harsh penalties for importing apples.

That path overhead's less dear, but cars and RVs just can't.
Freeze-frame by freeze-frame, long-take by long-take,

this passage by ferry scans a span too broad to drive,
too slow for wifi, textures defying all charts.

It begs reflection. Better than a cinema to get cool,
I buy time, spin it out, knitting yarns, sifting angles,

attitudes on a seascape oblivious. Shamelessly
I eavesdrop, it's everybody's spectacle. On the lip

of rogue waves, swell of complicit crests,
is the answer I question. What is the hold of cities?

For what gleaming lure do we sing aaah, aaah, swallow,
and raw from the maul of its barbs, swallow again?

VI

Foundering

Blowhole

It might be the name, ocean idea of waves
bathing the sky that misleads. Today I see how

I've missed the finale, distracted by each
spume-dragon. I know that plot. The spout discharging,

I don't release my breath. The spectre curls,
reverses, wallop coincides with my exhale. Belly-flop

on pink granite cheeks, a spanking smack.
Like showing off a dive as an unpracticed kid.

Or the hollow sound cried by an old slipper as it
whips young skin – no, forget that, pay attention here.

The cascade dribbles, flounces each curve with
solace, a sister's hug. Chortling now, the wave rejoins

the sheltering sea in the gulch where a pier stands
almost absolved of limbs, and a red skiff moors.

Secret

That summer we took a weatherboard cottage
      on Mount Desert Island
I was two, a turtle in my red hoodie, my Secret,
      having no word for invisible.
If only Dad had taken me in the big shiny boat,
      up-and-down on the green Atlantic.

The fishers were gone when through
      high dune grass I found the cove,
beach being swallowed by a giant-tongued ocean.
      I was its tadpole, backed against
the breathless cliff, my first unmarked grave.

I didn't yet have wings to reach that nook where
      wall meets ceiling, to suspend myself
spider-splayed above it all. Still I have no words
      for 'it all'. I was a bad girl –
a steady refrain, no need to worry them as I did.

Now, in a stroke, I'd rewrite that day, never
      to learn those bloated pink words,
'behave', 'stay with Mum', 'float'. I'd take more
      smother of that east coast fog,
leaving brine's itchy sting and a fishy smell
      as Maine's sole residues.

The ship-breaker

This shore at full throttle's a last port of call. Vessels die young,
    fatigue's a freight. Some let fly
their propellers, running high on the shingle, if anything runs

without legs. Ship-breakers have legs. They wade into slurries
    of oil, chemicals, bilge that seeps round
incontinent hulls. Sinewy arms harvest metals, liquids,

stained blankets that smell of bodies long since slogging
    on some other deck. Siddiqi wields
his height, climbs and cuts, cuts and climbs, sings loudly

for courage, as the gas torch hisses, bites through steel
    no blade could tackle. He hates the risk,
is glad for work, the steaming dahl that gives rice joy.

His kiddies, drum-tummied, doze by day – school uniforms
    are too dear, a real meal's a stretch even for festivals.
In one blink   a wall   falls away,

bamboo scaffolding   peels from the bulkhead.
    Under slabs   men and tools are scrambled,   hammered
        into sandy heaps.   Siddiqi's legs   are severed.

'Clean,' they say, 'lucky.' Mates lay him   in a blanket
    between cooking pots,   in his room   with toy windows,
        red curtains.   He'll never   work again,

never squat to empty, wash himself. Dignity's last hinge is broken –
    he'll pray to Allah   on his back. Now Siddiqi's   really learning submission.
        In Dhaka's tips,   small hands harvest   what grace sends –

odd plastic sandals,   high-smelling rags,   oceans of bags, containers
    without lids, lids free-wheeling,   whatever sells.   This life
        is the art of tiny increment.   Here Siddiqi's kids work,   see themselves,

bits blown clear of purpose. But they're saving,   a secret, to buy
    a cutting torch. The boys will learn   ship-breaking,
        so there's dahl for all, Father too. Home is sweeter

with his rich singing, sonorous, even joyous.
    Walls, the luff of the red-curtained
window, and hope remain, steady last trestles.

Hey poem!

You – beachcomber, larrikin, you know the inside of wrecks,
hulks, vinegar-oily, corrosive swill, snags of shonky-sharp.

So why choose me? You are a searchlight that trains on me,
x-rays me through. Thanks for that. To you, my body's

naked, exposing all that I am, am not. Yet you set me
to revel 'I am, I am', in my holey jumper. Don't be cross.

We owe this much to moths – antenna envy. Any flutter
at life's more than innate. Their muse-dust is the dandruff

of scales, price of touch or flight. Our grail is play, laughter
on its trampoline. Some say we can't live on a vista,

you see views, like humour, as food groups. You say you sit
lightly with words, your nibbles are fangs to four a.m. poets.

Help me say touch needs motion, say art delivers us clear
and earthy like tea fragrant-green with roast rice,

one sip a sense-meal. Even legends need poetry vessels,
verges to clutch, groovy shores, foot and hand holds.

Allied with you, poem, shell-pools shine louder, hues dilate,
saturate even the desert-bogged, the reclusive, the detainee.

Let's chant to typhoons, curry rust, frisk sand's prisms,
gargle old tales, new names, the salt of each elemental grain.

Knots for beginners

To make a carrick or sheepshank, stevedore
or monkey's fist – take the bitter end
in hand, loop over another with the working end,

weave over and under to form a third loop. Repeat.
Pass through loops following the first round
three or four times. A whipping will stabilise results.

Prolong knots extend, twist, overlap outer bights.
Tied as a cylinder, this knot's a useful woggle.
Seizings will preserve its flat shape,

prevent slippage, which is a risk. A decorative knot
secures lanyards, adds padding to protect decks,
gunwales from rub and impact of quay and cargo.

My notes –
    The bitter end in hand, the rest is easy, loops and twists
    show me familiar shores for the first time.
    Like ripe plums, seldom do I divine which fruit is bad.

    It's good to get a lead on life by prior experience
    but instructions and diagrams reveal
    so little of knurls at hand, I'm never on the right page.

    Loss and grief are withstood when braced, a hollow pole
    holds bones and ashes, pain and sweetness,
    in vertical prayer. A column of blue butterflies may serve.

    Whipping sounds harsh, is only the swaddling of vulnerable
    limbs. Risk lies in finding which end's
    susceptible. My gall is to go unarmed, porous to kindness,

and then. Subsiding results from transport, mud, proximity.
I want traction in love and friendship,
though wadding's a fair salve for rasp. In the case of a heart,

do not cosset but cherish callouses softly amassed,
romp by caper. Stinger suits
are popular in a range of bruise-and-cruise patterns.

'I'll see you then'

Last sailing of MV *Sewol*, 2014

i. 'Once in a Lifetime': Jeju Island brochure

Visit famous Jeju Island, South Korea. Climb the breathtaking
Hallasan Volcano. Feast your eyes on the opal lake,
it might make them blue! Inhale Gotjawal Forest,
its six thousand species. Stroll our black and white beaches
…but remember, phones immersed in salt water corrode.

Jeju boasts three world-heritage sites, fifteen million charmed
visitors each year. Most come from China.
Feast your taste buds on crispy black pig, pumpkin duck.
In Loveland's sculpture garden, plan your honeymoon (18+ only)
…though children don't know that need for after-balm.

Or warm your heart at the Teddy Bear Museum.
See for yourself the world's smallest teddy, 4.5 millimetres tall!
Admire the grace of Seongnimgyo Arch Bridge,
or face your cold fears in the world's longest lava tube.
…unless you meet all your fears before reaching Jeju.

Relax on roaring beaches or find your courage in the surf.
Cheongjeyeong Falls will leave you gasping as it drops
deep into ocean. Meet your inner fish at Jeju Water World
and Mud Festival. Breathtaking views, just imagine –
…knowing you always travel at your own risk.

You'll never feel more alive than on Sunrise Peak.
Jeju Folk Village teaches respect for our past. Visit O'Sulloc
Tea Museum for indoor garden perfection, its tea store
will refresh your soul with blossom fragrant gifts
…but if only your soul's left, you won't crave little cups of tea.

ii. Danwon High School trip

It's a routine ferry run down to Jeju Island. Lifeboats hang
like cheeky lungs, sky lanterns, festival-ready. Children board
in a rip of chatter and giggles. Backpacks collide.
'Watch out, captain!' they joke, leaning into holiday mode.

Kpop resounds off bulkheads, bunks are swapped. Ravenous,
with nerves, they tear open sweet potato crisps, chocolate Peperos.
Soon Happy Promise Custard Cake litters the carpet, chased
by Chilsung Soda Pop, as if a long night weren't yawning.

Officials have slept smugly while MV *Sewol* had an overhaul,
cargo volume doubled. Nylon rope's cheaper
than chain to secure a load, if nothing happens. Stacked high
now with Lego containers, she's been made a play ship.

Inspectors work faster from shore, smooth business.
Sailors round Incheon Harbour prefer a greasy night in port.
This ferry alone puts to sea. Master Lee's a relief skipper.
Has he heard whispers of faked documents, ill-trained crew?

At breakfast, students laugh   into their soup. Dumpling islands,
lotus leaf rice cakes,   cabbage and spring onion   make
a seascape   tilting dramatically,   slopping   across the table.
The ferry's heeling sharply,   turning. Currents run strong.

Under force, vehicles, containers   break free,   slide,
        batter bulkheads. Water gushes   through mangled
cargo doors. One worried passenger   calls authorities,
        who scold him   for not having   the ship's position.

Crew radio SOS   in slow motion,
        don't begin   evacuation.
        Local fishers   scoop up   passengers
                leaping   overboard.

MV *Sewol*'s on her side   when the Coast Guard arrives   40 minutes later.
    Master Lee   is rescued first   in his professional   navy underpants,
then twenty-two crew. Seven staff remain on board. Land-based advisors
    prioritise: 'passengers   must form   orderly queues   to disembark.'

In cabin 671, mattresses fit   between short bunk partitions
    padding the new cant   of a steel floor. Giggles punctuate sobs.
Clammy hands clutch. Someone has hiccups. The door has risen,
    a rectangular moon lit by   emergency floodlights. Nothing is absurd.

Government divers   are unskilled,   ill-equipped   for deep dives.
    Civilians   plunge in,   too often   for the heart.
Salvage is blocked by politics. After the PM's impeachment,   three years on
    Sewol's raised. Mobile phones   and bones are retrieved.

Two hundred and fifty Danwon children
miss school, Jeju Island and the rest of life.
One diver, a vice-principal, and the ship's owner
                          suicide.

iii. Last words

(video-recorded, SMS texted, voiced by phone)
'The ship is leaning. Are we becoming a Titanic?'
    'This is fun. We're going to make the news with this.
    Here, take a selfie to remember this day.'

'What's the captain doing? Help! Help!'
    'We're all sticking together in here.'
        'Are the teachers safe somewhere?'

Announcement:
'Ladies and gentlemen, please confirm your lifejackets are tied!
Danwon High School students, you must remain in your cabins.'

'What about you?' 'Don't worry,
    I'll get one for myself.' 'Oh, look,
        they're jumping into the sea!'

'I just want to see my mum.'
    'I'm so scared, so scared. Save us!'
        'Little sister, never take a school trip like this!'

Announcement:
'Danwon High School students must remain in your cabins.
Hang on to available pillars.'

'This is crazy! Like the subway accident.
    They told people to stay put – only those
        who didn't follow orders survived.'

'I don't want to die. I've a lot of animation movies
    I haven't watched.' 'I love you Mum and Dad.
        I may not get another chance to say it.'

'I'm with friends. Too many people are in the corridor.'
    'My friends, if I ever did anything wrong to you, please
        forgive me.' 'This looks like the end. I love you.'

'Don't worry, we're gonna live. I'll see you then.'

VII

Pilot Station

Subject to change

Maritime forecast is variable.
Storm warning in effect.
Wind southeast thirty-five to forty-five knots
increasing to south forty-five to fifty-five
late overnight then diminishing
to southwest twenty-five to thirty-five near noon.
Wind becoming northeast in the evening.

Seas two to three metres
building to three to five near midnight
except five to seven over southeastern sections
in the morning and afternoon.
Rain and fog banks becoming snow.
Visibility one kilometre or less.
Temperatures near zero.

    Expected shipping is subject to change.

Conception Light, bulk carrier, departure 2115,
Origin port of Longview to port of Bluff,
Flag: Hong Kong

Glorious Plumeria, bulk carrier, departure 0930,
Origin port of Komatsushima to port of Singapore,
Flag: Panama

Burra, commercial towage, arrival 0900,
Origin port of Geelong to port of Geelong,
Flag: Australia

Statesman, barge, departure 0845,
Origin port of Grassy to port of Stanley,
Flag: Australia

Star Life, bulk carrier, arrival 1745,
Origin port of Newcastle to port of Melbourne,
Flag: Marshall Islands

Le Laperouse, passenger vessel, departure 1145,
Origin port of Grassy to Port Lincoln,
Flag: France

Subject to change. Subject, to change.

Late running lights

My craft shows running lights,
green, red and white

solace to each other
in nights of night.

Green's my calculator,
frontal lobes wary, heavy

with anchor-chain logic,
refusing the pull to levitate,

billow into spinnaker silk.
Red's to port, left-handed,

right-brained, tickles peppery
ripe reflections,

shadows' renderings, where
truth and passion wave

wet spaghetti strands
between me and that beacon,

that ferry, that newborn moon.
White light's my kindle,

inspiriting a now beyond
vigilance, where tints and tones

converge at the watery junction
of amazement. This light

lends me spine enough
through squalls

and backscattering stillness,
steady, awaiting dawn's trickle.

A marked man

Emanuel Griffin, Thames River pilot transported for life, arrived in Tasmania in 1806. A pilot on the Tamar Estuary, freed in the 1820s, he serviced Low Head Pilot Station until his death in 1844.

Griff is a Thames fisher with a sweet-salty bloodline,
a marked man. A skiff with no name, catch of fishy provenance
are offences enough to be transported for life.

Any griffin wants hybrid being, fresh with saline, edgy
where sea and stone and sand converge in a hubbub
of gurgles and dirges. In this Tamar estuary, ships founder,

Port Dalrymple's promise wallows. The aunties,
who breathe every river song, whisper seafood to hand,
call for a wind change, slip clear of white menace.

Theirs is resistance to unwelcome traffic, nautical lynching,
drowning. Here Griff pilots, still marked. Convict appetites
are harnessed to constraint. Griff relieves sailors drifting

fast toward disbelief in any lord of the seas. His boatmen
row him out, he scales the rope ladder. Safe passage
is his power, incoming goods, settlers' pianolas and brats,

hats to meet the king's man, scientists' samples, chronometers.
Tables turned, he farewells crops, wool, the king's mail,
whatever ground and town can yield, until the north lies

in Griff's smooth hands, his the official ears of the sea.
Yet he's marked, not for gifts, crimes-alleged, but a small tattoo
is recorded. History's an incurious distillation of persons.

On Hebe Reef

RIP
brig *Hebe* (1808)
barque *Phillip Oakden* (1851)
cutter *Mariner* (1861)
schooner *Jane and Elizabeth* (1867)
barque *Asterope* (1883)
steam ship *Esk* (1886)
ketch *Windward* (1890)
barque *Eden Holme* (1907)
ore carrier *Iron Baron* (1995)

Steel grinds shrill on rock, shudders, tosses everything, bruising
    the galley's iceberg lettuce, gimballed stove frantic.
That winter day the pilot, Damo or Bruce, boards *Iron Baron*
    already doomed, far-tangled in a surf of human micro-error.
Computer-guided ships, GPS, radar like gods, swap away mystery,

see all – reefs, sandbanks, hulls before impact, human flops.
    Yet boundaries of solid, liquid, gas, of health and hell remain.
Bass Strait's ghost ships still keen, 'beware *Hebe*'s last port'.
    Holding death close keeps the living well, some say.
In hindsight, calling wrecks romantic softened nostalgia for times

more kindly only in pace. Some boundaries are not worth pushing.
    All breath loses its beat in oil's superglue. Algae, plankton,
ancient peat bogs are pressed oozy under deadweight until
    that old seabed's drill-ruptured, pumped, piped, shipped,
fracked and blended back into our days. Colonies of penguins,

black swans, seals, cormorants smother under *Iron Baron*'s slick.
    'Black gold' by any name's toxic to feathers, beaks, lungs,
guts, gills, breath. Refused salvage, scuttled at sea, *Iron Baron* now
    lies rustless, deep in a munitions dump, all fossil follies,
as if beamed to another planet. But out-of-sight is not enough.

Micro-errors, micro plastics, micro-fragments claim small
    is nothing but we have satellites, microscopic eyes to see
inside, beyond, before. Still we play blind. The only poetry here
    is not accusation or affront – it's firm refusal of forces
that glibly annul this life, all its dainty cellular magic.

Pendant buoy 1830–1960

Pilot Station Museum, Low Head, Tasmania

Cone-top red and white, no light, she was only a gull's rest
on a glad wild ride, ridge to rift to ridge. An elongated football,
two tall-men tall, she's jerseyed white with red stripes.
Acrylic paint provides plastic cohesion for Huon pine oils,
repelling crustacean civilisations and worm tropes.
Lug big as a head, port-barrel bands are a whalebone corset
in reverse, stout round the middle, better adapted than
Barbie's fragile hourglass. Those hoops still hold fast against
dirty weather, echoes of threats, dereliction on Hebe's Reef.
No bold bell warded off crunch, groan, cries of wet demise.
Too great a prize to leave on a reef? What then is precious?
Any time now a gust will tumble her crust, rust smithereens
beyond revival, onto roo-kempt lawns. Who will miss her?
Today she sits rakish, over-exposed to tourists who gawk past,
eyes only for hot scones and cream in the pinch-tight café.
Too long she guarded this estuary mouth, the silent screams
of pilots' wives, mewling flocks of baby Van Diemonians.

Beach bone

Eye sockets epic, her ridged face is long, a pointed
ivory relic. The brain box is eggshell porcelain that
light glows through – I wonder what ideas sparked here.

Expertise for leaves of bluish hues, black sheen,
frost-rimmed or dawn-glittered flutter? I see where
she breathed this salt-fresh air, nose tracking, sniffing.

This one skull chose me with its patina. Many wash up,
but why do pademelon bones rubble on this beach, among
mane-mounds of seagrass and bubble-weed entrails?

Shorter-nosed, I'm drawn to her tiny teeth like old steps,
sway-backed from fibrous wear. Is this the dawn
of my love for textiles and oral, tactile fixations?

Eight molars and bonded twins fill her upper jaw.
The downward segment protrudes six incisors, shaping
her sweet-lipped smile. She would have struggled

to floss, teeth packed tight, I know. We reach an age where
gums recede, hot drinks, ice cream hit a nerve. I blow
tepid the silver porridge-spoon her niece licks for breakfast.

Milk reminds this sweetie of lazy-pouch days, a front-row
seat for vaulting, rocking with mother's rhythms, heartbeat,
days and nights uncluttered beyond this-now-good.

Schoolhouse

Pilot Station Schoolhouse, Low Head, Tasmania

Steps from the boulder beach, two doors separate girls
from boys, as if plumbing matters more when bells ring,

funnelled into the same sweaty vestibule. Thirty-eight pegs
wait still at ten-to-the-hour for coats and caps. Bright sprites

bounded in, blue fingers, toes to thaw. Their feet paddled
these boards, polished each precious square nailhead.

In the cracks, flecks of dandruff, DNA, how long do they last?
Kids of pilots, coxes, the wives they sustained without breaking

– this is about plumbing – huddled on this bluestone beak,
jettisoned into Bass Strait's blend of hell and heaven.

A century of pupils cracked slates, mumbled in unison's
shelter at tongue-in-groove walls over grumbling tums.

Plumbing again. The few who read, read all four books, recited
them over and over to babes of babes. Shadowed by pox

and poverty, they never saw this handsome room
lime-washed clean, so still, echoing lap and lonely gull.

Their crude initials are gone with the benches for kindling.
In this museum-hotel, a pilot's wage wouldn't cover

our few austere nights. The lounge is supersized, mock-hessian
upholstery evoking an overfed mammoth. The electric fire

grins if you flick a switch – the master did, welts stood rosy
in queues. We're all flayed by the Roaring Forties' hiss,

unlike this flatscreen, silenced by a fingertip's remote decree. This morning's mine to write. The stainless lighthouse glows,

a rolling boil down the bench-wharf. Tea lubricates my neural pathways, unscrews my fingertips so they may drip words.

Night sailing

The boat of myself
is red-canvas rigged,
tacks tight, drum-taut

to the wind, spars blow
free of dusty custom.
Racing a squall, flying's

the very next thing
to skimming on the tension
of a meniscus curve,

flexi-film beyond design.
I can't see the wind, but
know its cheek on my face.

Defying gravity,
pennants too stand boldly
apart from their stays.

This imperious draw
I can't withstand. I hurl on
in and into this rousing brew.

Brush

A few days of remote are written in postcards
from forgotten items. Today's might have tamed my hair –

> on its own wild fling along this wind-hewn
> shore. But 'brush' sounds flirty, too kind. I'm cross.

After a crude finger-comb, reckoning again here
are no shops, I feel a walk could air my topknot,

> unkempt nest that can't resist Roaring Forties' directives.
> Yet thin air offers no easy passage to a body plotting

a contrary course. Limewashed curves of leading lights entice,
She Oak Point and Middle Channel, whose columns glow by day.

> Cylinders of rubble, chess pieces knobbed, at twilight
> these twin minarets turn sacred lanterns. Their mirrors

breed light from one flame, night's kindest deception.
Leading lights in alignment, steam ahead, you've a safe course

> to cross this petulant mouth. Would that I were
> a shaven pink buoy. Bobbing glad and mad,

a fluoro bathing-cap might distract me from
my own skull spume. Then I could tail all day

> these ducks on parade, his and hers preening haughty,
> smug in their hairsprayed svelte-feathered coifs.

Ship in a bottle

For Dad (b. 1929–)

See the boy at his bench, crafting this vessel in a vessel in some other vessel to sail beyond his wars, dock at my sill. This clipper has cruised eighty years

in her bottle, three masts raffish. Glass sides have magnified English rain, Canadian frost-ferns, Tasmanian mist. If a bottled message comes to hand,

look in through the scrim. See the boy's mother – I have her faulty ears. Head scarfed, she's off to Willaston's chemist for a bottle of remedy.

The boy's chest may wheeze, autumn coal-burning smells of snow, Christmas, things not yet come to pass. I have his lungs, leathery bellows, broad cough.

Or will she bring syrup from honeyed shores, green-pink cheek of pistachios, purple figs where it rains only rosewater? Sure to cleanse the English gut,

the bottle's spare. See the boy, I have his eyes. He chooses box, a creamy wood, tight rings, fine grain too dense for fuel or floating. His young hand churns

the wheel, steadies the helm, micro-drilling allows no error. From some Cornish artery, men dug tin, drew out hairs of sunrise. The boy shapes hinges, steps

the masts. Filaments flow and pull in unison. His knots, lashings, make a string rigging from Manchester's hundred thousand spindles, grey with din. After

sliding folded, tight through the birth canal – we all do – the hull is glued down. At dawn he will tug one trailing thread, umbilical cinch to his cathedral.

Spanish cork fills the neck, harvested in nine-year rites, cohorts share seasons of nakedness, green bark, caramel hatching. The boy's accented children will

be fed on old worlds teeming with new dreams. As sailcloth softens, so his skin, but his vision orbits on, a sometimes-brimming vessel of brightness.

VIII

Bruny Island Ferry

Mirage

This ferry floats on its own pool of shadow,
double bill, second hull, yang lending speed to yin

on the beam. We're running hard to Roberts Point
as if something pressing were happening there,

school vacation waning to a cuticle, paddocks wavering,
heat-smirched strawberry-blonde. Gulls mill vague

above the channel tasting for hints of change,
beads of windchill. Out there, a dinghy's marooned

on a chasmic mirror, sails drooping tame
and flabby. Another mirage. This day's luminous,

a carousel, cheeky ember begging perverse touch.

Nautical draughts

Six large adults board with a large child clutching
a small screen. It's Gran's birthday.
They mint them young here. No older than me,

she's transparent, light tap-dancing on water.
Don't mention candles on the cake
but this may be her last. Good to spend the day

afloat, carried. Practising. Return fare's free on foot,
and the shore café serves
a hero's mound of chips. Gran doesn't eat chips.

Her son rabbits on about engines to the high-viz
skipper, whose goatee is unmoved
by the word-flood. He's sanitising chrome seats,

roping them off with glossy white nylon. We're all
learning to keep space,
practice distancing. If only rope could do the job.

Abruptly Skip stands tall, bursts into 'Happy Birthday'.
Larrikin, his aria breaks tedium,
pops a cork into Motor-Mouth. Spray bottles, damp rags

stored away, our skipper strides forward, origami-folds
himself into his throne. He's kinged
again, launches another round of ship-to-shore, gliding

over water, sure winner in the tick-tack ferry game
of nautical draughts. Some of us,
virus-flustered, are still discerning the rules, first move.

Hydraulic force

No charge on foot to ride this ferry, trailers
pay eighty-five dollars. Cheaper to be
a whole copse of legs, chubby, sunburnt,
knobbly, varicose. Queues too have their costs.

To find a course, stem the tide of futures
unknown, I have long craved an oracle,
scarlet needle hovering in a crystal dome,
beaming brass binnacle of guidance –

any firm handle on tangles. Later, I see how
following, life's trailer-days lacked texture,
tasted fake as green jelly, banana icy poles,
false as a pulse raised by a screen game.

I struggle with slopping horizons, reluctant
to know that nothing stays put, a ferry afloat
is as real as destinations get. DIY proves less
trustworthy than holding a steady course

on random kindness, love's bubbles.
This whole being human's hydraulic, fluids
under pressure. Yet swills of delight are sure
promises, honest frolics of now and then.

Deckhands

Between casting off and landing, deckhands
lounge fluorescent on the aft bridge.

One sits in the vinyl lazy-boy, legs over arms,
a new nautical knot. He's gawky, as if this

were his first time at scouts. The crew trail
our magnet, double-ender ferry, drawing us back

to harbour, homing with unswerving force.
Hands are all about timing, fronting quays,

sensitive zones at the right moment. The bump
of the vessel on the wharf's not lost on dogs

dozing in ute trays who, unmoved, perk up just
one ear. The gates pour out foot traffic, a slick

of metallic vehicles, rainbow-high on oil.
Perfect timing for hands, a smoko and long black.

Picture postcard

In this postcard, three ferries tack
out from Kettering. Shiny-fast metallic,
our indoor-outdoor viewing deck's

mainly for tourists with large
phone memories. Locals are offhand,
sit crammed in their cars feigning

disinterest. We cross the older ferries,
speed meets working belles –
sheep and lumber, tankers swollen

with petrol, sagging udders empty
of milk, sometimes a prefab house,
campervan with dead sparkplugs

needing a push. We're colorised
in post-production, but postcards
from this edge can't capture it.

No greeting conveys the vivid pop,
d'Entrecasteaux's screaming blue,
how one channel's tiny patch of sky

could be so perfectly bottomless.

Our Kettering

Our Kettering's named for a humour-drained landlubber's
    town in Northamptonshire.
In that Kettering, the dole's the go, the tanneries are gone,
    even the convicts have sailed.
Shedding last lasts, the footwear industry shipped offshore,
    left foot to Malaysia, right to Korea.
Now theft's called shrinkage, two left feet are common in KL.

Bare feet are no surfie luxury but shame and pain.
    Now footwear's made quick-cheap,
synthetics heat-bonded, oil-based, called vegan but don't
    chew them. Flashy zips shout 'non-functional'.
Most footwear skips the stores, flicks off
    by courier to bargain buyers curating
home piers, fast-fashion catwalks, then zips to the tip.

In old Kettering they know, some highways rush to hubs
    of despond and despair.
The Domesday Survey in 1086 valued the whole town,
    home of Ketter's people, at £11, too little
for a pub lunch at the Beeswing. It'll do for takeaway roast
    and gravy on a bap. Why not sail straight
for pudding, lemon sponge or Eton mess with cream?

Our Kettering hosts dozens of yachts, trophy holes where
    the money goes. Most rarely leave
their slips. Kettering's a commute from Hobart's CBD.
    In truth, with credit maxed,
everyday belongs to the bank. The high life has its lines
    but they flick and sting, drift from reach.
In pinched straits, tides of delusion rip fast and deep.

Sunday at the Beeswing

Pub in Kettering, UK, from online reviews

'My family always goes down, a lovely lad takes our order.'
'It rains every Sunday on that terrace.' 'There's an atmosphere

with the manager. Seriously.' 'The Beeznees, orders in a flash
by a cracking guy'. 'Excellent refurb. Almost home. No better.'

'Amazing fact, farther-in-law's wasn't last or late.'
'Glad me and Nan decided to go somewhere different.'

'Great Sunday spot if you need someplace to go on Sundays.'
'Jesus Christ stopped here as it looked pleasant.'

'Car park never has many cars in it, tells you something.'
'All the buzz.' 'Lost my pink umbrella there with its spots.

They must of gave it to the charity shop.' 'The girl behind
the bar looks like she doesn't want to be there.'

'The Beeswing is dear.' 'Got served more roast potatoes,
Yorkie and gravy. We'll be back for more more!'

Missing out

Loading again, steel plates grumble,
bridge-to-barge grinds hollow, warm-up noises
comfort. Gran and her progeny are gone,
off to the cafe for more chips.
They'll sit this round out. I guess festivities
progress, with lashings of local colour,

generous squirts of tomato sauce. A red Jeep
rolls on, racks and boot bursting with bikes
and surfboards. Active people, this is no day trip.
The five sit windows down, not enticed
to scale twelve stairs, ogle delicious
from my eyrie of pure nonesuch.

I am open-mouthed, salivating, agog
with ferry fever but I do understand. Despite
best intentions, compressed air loudly loosed
by lighthouses, phone alarms sounding bells,
best steamboat mimicry, every alert –
ever alert, I miss so many boats.

Albatross

An albatross observes us from its height, suspicious of ships
with no catch. This arvo the antipodean Aegean's turquoise-studded,

diamonds roll south on crests. I cannot grab them to swirl
in my mouth like unpopped kernels. I hadn't heard of this hissing,

thumping Great Southern Ocean till lately, deaf to its fight and roar.
I can dismiss gaps as northern bias, or a seventies education

with victims like grammar, but it's ignorance. My urban kind
doesn't know what sand gets up to, how itinerant one grain can be.

Easier to imagine a bright blanket pilling in a yurt on the steppes.
In truth, one grain of sand circles all round, may return to our beach

like salmon to spawn, as if salmon and sand share dreams.
Albatross I met once in Coleridge. Now I know a single wing

might cast a vessel in shadow. On long hauls, albatross coast,
lock their shoulders, circle this over-inflated planet at a go,

mythical only in their truth. But it's a terse flight to natural history
museums' extinct galleries. We'll put them away like all other

megafauna. Some do like history repeating itself. Birds' demise
in longline nets, we dismiss as 'nature'. Like 'roadkill',

words that come with a shrug. I'm watching, learning. Albatross
are lonely, sooty, wandering, laughing mollymawks. They hunt

by smell, measure flight speed by nostril gauge. Killing
an albatross may jinx you. Who can argue for felling a giant

just to have a go at her bean-stock? Post-moderns wield our
power-word, 'feral', as if gods bother with junk, billions of genetic

instructions for supersized lives, no more than epic 3D misprints.

The limits

On deck, they take selfies,
tick-tick with mock aperture,
only shutter sound effects.
Rome, Paris, Kettering,
worlds pile on shoulders.

They can make action still,
suspend leap and cascade,
but know better than expecting
to capture liquid magic
untamed in its free slide and sway.

No words can spell its name,
no pixel can grasp voluble's
heyday. Surges augment,
drips in flight, fluid's fine fury,
bold oceanic zeniths.

Bruny Island

Roberts Point again. Still no sign of Roberts, maybe
he's out checking nets. Engines reverse,
we nudge the pier, crew make fast, lower the bridge.

Cars clear their throats, slide clunkety off and up
the hill. From the upper deck I review their options,
too early for B&Bs or serious whisky-tasting.

Campsites are chockers on holiday Saturdays,
praying's not worth your breath unless it's also raining.
But our chilly surf's always up for those who do.

The cheese factory's logo is a pair of old gumboots,
down-to-earth, hints of hippy unrestrained by orthodox
caseiculture. In truth, laughing cows

have cornered the market on ravishing real estate.
Cheese factory coffee's served fragrant in gum shade,
minds on cheese, fruity and piquant spread thick,

runny on just-baked sourdough. Ferry-riders don't know
the lushest isle can be a bread desert. They're in time
for the bite, resolute crust, glorious sponge of fresh loaves

smooth with the salt of local butter, amber of leatherwood
honey. It's one island version of shelter under
the sublime's umbrella – these are heaven's denim skies.

Bucket list

The ferryman's a silver bikie when
he's not piloting his high speed ferry, tells me he dreams
of seeing the Isle of Man. Not its ferries,

not Thomas the Tank Engine but TT bike races
top his bucket list. I say they're loud, they moan, two high-
pitched weeks of whine cancel notions

of poetry or thought. That voice of old bikes
is his passion, he confesses. I don't mention ancient stones,
cottages wrapped in foam rubber,

humpbacked fairy bridges lying in wait,
how I hate 'collateral damage'. Every year's a toxic lark,
Sunday riders, chiselled roads grasping cliffs,

hairpin bends, air thick with beer
and testosterone. The ferryman's a bikie charmer but
there's no race in lockdown, bucket lists

will wait, serve as bailers for another year
or six. Lives may be extended unawares. Here queues
for his ferry lengthen, three lanes,

pressing hot, raging for Bruny's calm.
We've black and white empty beaches, albino wallabies,
still pools and sheltering bays, blasts

of Antarctic wind that slam the lighthouse,
shrieking surf, all the wind in your hair you could dream.
It's that good and more here at home.

Does this zen fail our ferryman?
Is it bloodsport he needs? Or human confirmation?
I don't mention how Manx coffee will disappoint.

White lies

Funny, the care we take, these surfboards wear their own sleek
coats. Nairana, Mirambeena, Moongalba, are ferry-names,
tokens of respect for First People. Truganini crossed just
this stretch. Perhaps in a possum coat, no cover enough when
convict woodchoppers spied her. We can't know if the worst

is true, her friends beheaded, convicts raped her here on her reed
boat. Did they tear her open, assault her soul? So long ago,
we can't know. Yet on Invasion Day, we do recall, celebrate
First Fleet heroics, fireworks marking fire-stick shootings,
massacres in so many Blackman's Creeks, Murdering Gullies,

places gone cruelly silent. Sparks fly, bang, bang, lest we forget –
cheers! So much joy we want to numb it. Not forgetting
pink saviour-boy Robinson's mission. One photo tells all,
Trugannini's eyes are deadly, fiery, though she's hobbled
by black satin. Her losses are worse than death. We do know –

the worst is true. How to forget what we never wanted to learn?
Damper and didjes, bush tucker, are not the whole story, not
this story at all. 'Welcome to Country' we tell ourselves,
pay elders to say. So dance! Dance! We've already taken over,
stripped the land of so much earth and starry wisdom.

We've dug it out, blown it up. Funny, now we're scared
of bushfires, floods. Our clumsy, bloody civilising
purged tongues and teachings we too needed, expertise on land,
water care, on life and living here. Remember this – hope
to fully belong was wiped out by white deeds and white lies.

Long weekend

Swell and wake, warp and heave meet here,
on this bay-brisk edge. Rattling ferries return empty,
weary, levitating on surreal surface tension at this
thin end of Saturday. Jersey barriers of worry fail
to outweigh enchantment, the magic still unspools.

Long weekends know their own desperate flutter,
miracles, landings. Is it pure illusion, pesto spread
on wedges lolling over hills, into vales of rocket forest?
Are rivulets pebbled with feta, hay bales pepperoni-zesty?
My mouth's indecent, harvest whispers so sensuous.

But enough feasting. Time to join the Channel Highway.
I'm tracking gratitude on fingers and toes, rolling back
to my surburban nest – one more green Colorbond roof,
gables folded in awe, eyes glazed in golden worship.
Again this watery home leans my willing pen to prayer.

About the poet

Pamela Leach is a proze-winning Tasmanian poet who engages culture, social justice, migration, environment and spirituality in her writing. Her poetry is known for its imagery, humour, compassion and irony. She has been published in journals including *Island*, *Quadrant*, *Bramble*, *The Mozzie*, *Forty South*, *Studio* and *Poetry in the Hospital*, and in two collections.

Growing up in Canada, Pamela swam early to equip her for boating, first sailing at age seven. She enjoyed wilderness canoe-tripping, dinghy cruising and served on square-rigged training vessels (tall ships) as petty officer. In water, boats and ships, Pamela found an interface with worlds natural and spiritual. Boats are seen by the poet as significant social and cultural vessels. She is an advocate for ferries and all forms of public transit.

Lyric storytelling is central to seagoing cultures. Exploring Canadian waterways, the Irish Sea, the West African coast and Tasmania, she has learned to deeply value water and landscapes, birds, sail craft, and stories. She has resided in Europe, West Africa and the United States. She migrated to Tasmania with her son Paul in 2010. Pamela holds a PhD in Political Studies (York University, Toronto). She taught Politics, Social Science, History and Human Rights in Canadian universities.

Living with disability, Pamela finds poetry a creative passion that does not require fine-motor skill. For her, sound play, language and silence mediate shared experiences and foster trust. Capacity for communication and humour prove vital. Pamela has been active in the Religious Society of Friends (Quakers) for forty years. This is her debut poetry collection. She welcomes correspondence via pamela.leach@hotmail.com

www.ingramcontent.com/pod-product-compliance
Lightning Source LLC
Chambersburg PA
CBHW071354080526
44587CB00017B/3108